ONE LINE A DAY

A Five Year Memory Book

This One Line a Day journal is a simple way to write down a thought or memory each day.

As our lives are continuously busy and filled with everyday commitments, this quick and easy journal is a wonderful way to store all of those special and joyous moments, that we don't want to forget.

We wish you much happiness and joy for all the memories and adventures that lay ahead.

Happy journaling.

WILDER THOUGHTS

JANUARY 1

20......

_____

20......

_____

20......

_____

20......

_____

20......

JANUARY 2

20...... _____

_____

_____

_____

_____

20...... _____

_____

_____

_____

_____

20...... _____

_____

_____

_____

_____

20...... _____

_____

_____

_____

_____

20...... _____

_____

_____

_____

_____

JANUARY 3

20...... _____

_____

_____

_____

20...... _____

_____

_____

_____

20...... _____

_____

_____

_____

20...... _____

_____

_____

_____

20...... _____

_____

_____

_____

JANUARY 4

20......

_____

20......

_____

20......

_____

20......

_____

20......

_____

JANUARY 5

20......

20......

20......

20......

20......

JANUARY 6

20......

20......

20......

20......

20......

JANUARY 7

20...... _____

_____

_____

_____

_____

20...... _____

_____

_____

_____

_____

20...... _____

_____

_____

_____

_____

20...... _____

_____

_____

_____

_____

20...... _____

_____

_____

_____

_____

JANUARY 8

20......

20......

20......

20......

20......

JANUARY 9

20......

_____

20......

_____

20......

_____

20......

_____

20......

_____

JANUARY 10

20...... _____

_____

_____

_____

20...... _____

_____

_____

_____

20...... _____

_____

_____

_____

20...... _____

_____

_____

_____

20...... _____

_____

_____

_____

JANUARY 11

20......

20......

20......

20......

20......

JANUARY 12

20...... _____

_____

_____

_____

20...... _____

_____

_____

_____

20...... _____

_____

_____

_____

20...... _____

_____

_____

_____

20...... _____

_____

_____

_____

20......

_____

20......

_____

20......

_____

20......

_____

20......

_____

20...... _____

_____

_____

_____

_____

20...... _____

_____

_____

_____

_____

20...... _____

_____

_____

_____

_____

20...... _____

_____

_____

_____

_____

20...... _____

_____

_____

_____

_____

JANUARY 15

20...... _____

_____

_____

_____

20...... _____

_____

_____

_____

20...... _____

_____

_____

_____

20...... _____

_____

_____

_____

20...... _____

_____

_____

_____

JANUARY 16

20......

_____

20......

_____

20......

_____

20......

_____

20......

_____

JANUARY 17

20...... _____

_____

_____

_____

_____

20...... _____

_____

_____

_____

_____

20...... _____

_____

_____

_____

_____

20...... _____

_____

_____

_____

_____

20...... _____

_____

_____

_____

_____

JANUARY 18

20......

20......

20......

20......

20......

JANUARY 19

20......

_____

20......

_____

20......

_____

20......

_____

20......

_____

20...... _____

_____

_____

_____

_____

20...... _____

_____

_____

_____

_____

20...... _____

_____

_____

_____

_____

20...... _____

_____

_____

_____

_____

20...... _____

_____

_____

_____

_____

JANUARY 21

20...... _____
_____
_____
_____
_____

20...... _____
_____
_____
_____
_____

20...... _____
_____
_____
_____
_____

20...... _____
_____
_____
_____
_____

20...... _____
_____
_____
_____
_____

JANUARY 22

20...... _____

_____

_____

_____

_____

20...... _____

_____

_____

_____

_____

20...... _____

_____

_____

_____

_____

20...... _____

_____

_____

_____

_____

20...... _____

_____

_____

_____

_____

JANUARY 23

20......

_____

20......

_____

20......

_____

20......

_____

20......

_____

JANUARY 24

20...... _____
_____
_____
_____
_____

20...... _____
_____
_____
_____
_____

20...... _____
_____
_____
_____
_____

20...... _____
_____
_____
_____
_____

20...... _____
_____
_____
_____
_____

20...... _____
_____
_____
_____

20...... _____
_____
_____
_____

20...... _____
_____
_____
_____

20...... _____
_____
_____
_____

20...... _____
_____
_____
_____

JANUARY 26

20...... _____

_____

_____

_____

20...... _____

_____

_____

_____

20...... _____

_____

_____

_____

20...... _____

_____

_____

_____

20...... _____

_____

_____

_____

JANUARY 27

20...... _____

_____

_____

_____

_____

20...... _____

_____

_____

_____

_____

20...... _____

_____

_____

_____

_____

20...... _____

_____

_____

_____

_____

20...... _____

_____

_____

_____

_____

JANUARY 28

20...... _____

_____

_____

_____

_____

20...... _____

_____

_____

_____

_____

20...... _____

_____

_____

_____

_____

20...... _____

_____

_____

_____

_____

20...... _____

_____

_____

_____

_____

JANUARY 29

20...... _____

_____

_____

_____

_____

20...... _____

_____

_____

_____

_____

20...... _____

_____

_____

_____

_____

20...... _____

_____

_____

_____

_____

20...... _____

_____

_____

_____

_____

20......

20......

20......

20......

20......

JANUARY 31

20...... _____

_____

_____

_____

20...... _____

_____

_____

_____

20...... _____

_____

_____

_____

20...... _____

_____

_____

_____

20...... _____

_____

_____

_____

FEBRUARY 1

20...... _____

_____

_____

_____

_____

20...... _____

_____

_____

_____

_____

20...... _____

_____

_____

_____

_____

20...... _____

_____

_____

_____

_____

20...... _____

_____

_____

_____

_____

FEBRUARY 2

20...... _____

_____

_____

_____

20...... _____

_____

_____

_____

20...... _____

_____

_____

_____

20...... _____

_____

_____

_____

20...... _____

_____

_____

_____

FEBRUARY 3

20......

_____

20......

_____

20......

_____

20......

_____

20......

FEBRUARY 4

20...... _____

_____

_____

_____

20...... _____

_____

_____

_____

20...... _____

_____

_____

_____

20...... _____

_____

_____

_____

20...... _____

_____

_____

_____

FEBRUARY 5

20...... _____

_____

_____

_____

_____

20...... _____

_____

_____

_____

_____

20...... _____

_____

_____

_____

_____

20...... _____

_____

_____

_____

_____

20...... _____

_____

_____

_____

_____

FEBRUARY 6

20...... _____

20...... _____

20...... _____

20...... _____

20...... _____

FEBRUARY 7

20...... _____

_____

_____

_____

_____

20...... _____

_____

_____

_____

_____

20...... _____

_____

_____

_____

_____

20...... _____

_____

_____

_____

_____

20...... _____

_____

_____

_____

_____

FEBRUARY 8

20......

_____

20......

_____

20......

_____

20......

_____

20......

_____

FEBRUARY 9

20......

_____

20......

_____

20......

_____

20......

_____

20......

_____

FEBRUARY 10

20......

_____

20......

_____

20......

_____

20......

_____

20......

_____

FEBRUARY 11

20......

_____

20......

_____

20......

_____

20......

_____

20......

FEBRUARY 12

20...... _____

_____

_____

_____

20...... _____

_____

_____

_____

20...... _____

_____

_____

_____

20...... _____

_____

_____

_____

20...... _____

_____

_____

_____

FEBRUARY 13

20...... _____

_____

_____

_____

_____

20...... _____

_____

_____

_____

_____

20...... _____

_____

_____

_____

_____

20...... _____

_____

_____

_____

_____

20...... _____

_____

_____

_____

_____

FEBRUARY 14

20……

20……

20……

20……

20……

FEBRUARY 15

20......

_____

_____

_____

_____

_____

20......

_____

_____

_____

_____

_____

20......

_____

_____

_____

_____

_____

20......

_____

_____

_____

_____

_____

20......

_____

_____

_____

_____

_____

20...... _____

_____

_____

_____

_____

20...... _____

_____

_____

_____

_____

20...... _____

_____

_____

_____

_____

20...... _____

_____

_____

_____

_____

20...... _____

_____

_____

_____

_____

FEBRUARY 17

20...... _____

_____

_____

_____

_____

20...... _____

_____

_____

_____

_____

20...... _____

_____

_____

_____

_____

20...... _____

_____

_____

_____

_____

20...... _____

_____

_____

_____

_____

FEBRUARY 18

20......

20......

20......

20......

20......

FEBRUARY 19

20......

_____

20......

_____

20......

_____

20......

_____

20......

_____

FEBRUARY 20

20......

20......

20......

20......

20......

FEBRUARY 21

20......

_____

_____

_____

_____

_____

20......

_____

_____

_____

_____

_____

20......

_____

_____

_____

_____

_____

20......

_____

_____

_____

_____

_____

20......

_____

_____

_____

_____

_____

FEBRUARY 22

20...... _____

_____

_____

_____

20...... _____

_____

_____

_____

20...... _____

_____

_____

_____

20...... _____

_____

_____

_____

20...... _____

_____

_____

_____

FEBRUARY 23

20...... _____

_____

_____

_____

_____

20...... _____

_____

_____

_____

_____

20...... _____

_____

_____

_____

_____

20...... _____

_____

_____

_____

_____

20...... _____

_____

_____

_____

_____

FEBRUARY 24

20...... _____

_____

_____

_____

20...... _____

_____

_____

_____

20...... _____

_____

_____

_____

20...... _____

_____

_____

_____

20...... _____

_____

_____

_____

FEBRUARY 25

20...... _____

_____
_____
_____
_____

20...... _____

_____
_____
_____
_____

20...... _____

_____
_____
_____
_____

20...... _____

_____
_____
_____
_____

20...... _____

_____
_____
_____
_____

FEBRUARY 26

20......

20......

20......

20......

20......

FEBRUARY 27

20......

_____

_____

_____

_____

_____

20......

_____

_____

_____

_____

_____

20......

_____

_____

_____

_____

_____

20......

_____

_____

_____

_____

_____

20......

_____

_____

_____

_____

_____

FEBRUARY 28

20......

_____

20......

_____

20......

_____

20......

_____

20......

_____

MARCH 1

20...... _____

_____

_____

_____

_____

20...... _____

_____

_____

_____

_____

20...... _____

_____

_____

_____

_____

20...... _____

_____

_____

_____

_____

20...... _____

_____

_____

_____

_____

MARCH 2

20......

20......

20......

20......

20......

MARCH 3

20......

_____

20......

_____

20......

_____

20......

_____

20......

_____

MARCH 4

20...... _____
_____
_____
_____

20...... _____
_____
_____
_____

20...... _____
_____
_____
_____

20...... _____
_____
_____
_____

20...... _____
_____
_____
_____

MARCH 5

20...... _____
_____
_____
_____
_____

20...... _____
_____
_____
_____
_____

20...... _____
_____
_____
_____
_____

20...... _____
_____
_____
_____
_____

20...... _____
_____
_____
_____
_____

MARCH 6

20......

20......

20......

20......

20......

MARCH 7

20...... _____

_____

_____

_____

_____

20...... _____

_____

_____

_____

_____

20...... _____

_____

_____

_____

_____

20...... _____

_____

_____

_____

_____

20...... _____

_____

_____

_____

_____

MARCH 8

20......

_____

20......

_____

20......

_____

20......

_____

20......

MARCH 9

20......

_____

_____

_____

_____

_____

20......

_____

_____

_____

_____

_____

20......

_____

_____

_____

_____

_____

20......

_____

_____

_____

_____

_____

20......

_____

_____

_____

_____

_____

MARCH 10

20...... _____

_____

_____

_____

_____

20...... _____

_____

_____

_____

_____

20...... _____

_____

_____

_____

_____

20...... _____

_____

_____

_____

_____

20...... _____

_____

_____

_____

_____

MARCH 11

20...... _____

_____

_____

_____

_____

20...... _____

_____

_____

_____

_____

20...... _____

_____

_____

_____

_____

20...... _____

_____

_____

_____

_____

20...... _____

_____

_____

_____

_____

MARCH 12

20...... _____

_____

_____

_____

_____

20...... _____

_____

_____

_____

_____

20...... _____

_____

_____

_____

_____

20...... _____

_____

_____

_____

_____

20...... _____

_____

_____

_____

_____

MARCH 13

20......
_____

20......
_____

20......
_____

20......
_____

20......
_____

MARCH 14

20...... _____

20...... _____

20...... _____

20...... _____

20...... _____

MARCH 15

20...... _____
_____
_____
_____
_____

20...... _____
_____
_____
_____
_____

20...... _____
_____
_____
_____
_____

20...... _____
_____
_____
_____
_____

20...... _____
_____
_____
_____
_____

MARCH 16

20...... _____

_____

_____

_____

20...... _____

_____

_____

_____

20...... _____

_____

_____

_____

20...... _____

_____

_____

_____

20...... _____

_____

_____

_____

MARCH 17

20......
_____
_____
_____
_____
_____

20......
_____
_____
_____
_____
_____

20......
_____
_____
_____
_____
_____

20......
_____
_____
_____
_____
_____

20......
_____
_____
_____
_____
_____

MARCH 18

20...... _____

_____

_____

_____

20...... _____

_____

_____

_____

20...... _____

_____

_____

_____

20...... _____

_____

_____

_____

20...... _____

_____

_____

_____

MARCH 19

20......

20......

20......

20......

20......

MARCH 20

20...... _____

_____

_____

_____

_____

20...... _____

_____

_____

_____

_____

20...... _____

_____

_____

_____

_____

20...... _____

_____

_____

_____

_____

20...... _____

_____

_____

_____

_____

MARCH 21

20...... _____

_____

_____

_____

_____

20...... _____

_____

_____

_____

_____

20...... _____

_____

_____

_____

_____

20...... _____

_____

_____

_____

_____

20...... _____

_____

_____

_____

_____

MARCH 22

20...... _____

_____

_____

_____

_____

20...... _____

_____

_____

_____

_____

20...... _____

_____

_____

_____

_____

20...... _____

_____

_____

_____

_____

20...... _____

_____

_____

_____

_____

MARCH 23

20...... _____

_____

_____

_____

_____

20...... _____

_____

_____

_____

_____

20...... _____

_____

_____

_____

_____

20...... _____

_____

_____

_____

_____

20...... _____

_____

_____

_____

_____

MARCH 24

20...... _____

_____

_____

_____

_____

20...... _____

_____

_____

_____

_____

20...... _____

_____

_____

_____

_____

20...... _____

_____

_____

_____

_____

20...... _____

_____

_____

_____

_____

MARCH 25

20......

_____

_____

_____

_____

20......

_____

_____

_____

_____

20......

_____

_____

_____

_____

20......

_____

_____

_____

_____

20......

_____

_____

_____

_____

MARCH 26

20......

_____

20......

_____

20......

_____

20......

_____

20......

MARCH 27

20...... _____

_____

_____

_____

_____

20...... _____

_____

_____

_____

_____

20...... _____

_____

_____

_____

_____

20...... _____

_____

_____

_____

_____

20...... _____

_____

_____

_____

_____

MARCH 28

20...... _____
_____
_____
_____
_____

20...... _____
_____
_____
_____
_____

20...... _____
_____
_____
_____
_____

20...... _____
_____
_____
_____
_____

20...... _____
_____
_____
_____
_____

MARCH 29

20......

_____

_____

_____

_____

_____

20......

_____

_____

_____

_____

_____

20......

_____

_____

_____

_____

_____

20......

_____

_____

_____

_____

_____

20......

_____

_____

_____

_____

_____

MARCH 30

20...... _____
_____
_____
_____
_____

20...... _____
_____
_____
_____
_____

20...... _____
_____
_____
_____
_____

20...... _____
_____
_____
_____
_____

20...... _____
_____
_____
_____
_____

MARCH 31

20...... _____

_____

_____

_____

_____

20...... _____

_____

_____

_____

_____

20...... _____

_____

_____

_____

_____

20...... _____

_____

_____

_____

_____

20...... _____

_____

_____

_____

_____

APRIL 1

20...... _____

_____

_____

_____

_____

20...... _____

_____

_____

_____

_____

20...... _____

_____

_____

_____

_____

20...... _____

_____

_____

_____

_____

20...... _____

_____

_____

_____

_____

APRIL 2

20...... _____

_____

_____

_____

_____

20...... _____

_____

_____

_____

_____

20...... _____

_____

_____

_____

_____

20...... _____

_____

_____

_____

_____

20...... _____

_____

_____

_____

_____

APRIL 3

20......

_____

20......

_____

20......

_____

20......

_____

20......

_____

APRIL 4

20...... _____

_____

_____

_____

_____

20...... _____

_____

_____

_____

_____

20...... _____

_____

_____

_____

_____

20...... _____

_____

_____

_____

_____

20...... _____

_____

_____

_____

_____

APRIL 5

20...... _____

_____

_____

_____

20...... _____

_____

_____

_____

20...... _____

_____

_____

_____

20...... _____

_____

_____

_____

20...... _____

_____

_____

_____

APRIL 6

20......

20......

20......

20......

20......

APRIL 7

20...... _____

_____

_____

_____

_____

20...... _____

_____

_____

_____

_____

20...... _____

_____

_____

_____

_____

20...... _____

_____

_____

_____

_____

20...... _____

_____

_____

_____

_____

APRIL 8

20......

20......

20......

20......

20......

APRIL 9

20...... _____

_____

_____

_____

_____

20...... _____

_____

_____

_____

_____

20...... _____

_____

_____

_____

_____

20...... _____

_____

_____

_____

_____

20...... _____

_____

_____

_____

_____

20...... _____

_____

_____

_____

20...... _____

_____

_____

_____

20...... _____

_____

_____

_____

20...... _____

_____

_____

_____

20...... _____

_____

_____

_____

APRIL 11

20...... _____

_____

_____

_____

_____

20...... _____

_____

_____

_____

_____

20...... _____

_____

_____

_____

_____

20...... _____

_____

_____

_____

_____

20...... _____

_____

_____

_____

_____

APRIL 12

20...... _____

_____
_____
_____
_____

20...... _____

_____
_____
_____
_____

20...... _____

_____
_____
_____
_____

20...... _____

_____
_____
_____
_____

20...... _____

_____
_____
_____
_____

APRIL 13

20...... _____

_____

_____

_____

_____

20...... _____

_____

_____

_____

_____

20...... _____

_____

_____

_____

_____

20...... _____

_____

_____

_____

_____

20...... _____

_____

_____

_____

_____

APRIL 14

20......

_____

20......

_____

20......

_____

20......

_____

20......

_____

APRIL 15

20......

_____

20......

_____

20......

_____

20......

_____

20......

_____

20...... _____

_____

_____

_____

_____

20...... _____

_____

_____

_____

_____

20...... _____

_____

_____

_____

_____

20...... _____

_____

_____

_____

_____

20...... _____

_____

_____

_____

_____

APRIL 17

20...... _____

_____

_____

_____

20...... _____

_____

_____

_____

20...... _____

_____

_____

_____

20...... _____

_____

_____

_____

20...... _____

_____

_____

_____

APRIL 18

20......

_____

20......

_____

20......

_____

20......

_____

20......

APRIL 19

20...... _____

_____

_____

_____

20...... _____

_____

_____

_____

20...... _____

_____

_____

_____

20...... _____

_____

_____

_____

20...... _____

_____

_____

_____

APRIL 20

20...... _____

_____

_____

_____

_____

20...... _____

_____

_____

_____

_____

20...... _____

_____

_____

_____

_____

20...... _____

_____

_____

_____

_____

20...... _____

_____

_____

_____

_____

20......

_____

20......

_____

20......

_____

20......

_____

20......

_____

APRIL 22

20...... _____

_____

_____

_____

_____

20...... _____

_____

_____

_____

_____

20...... _____

_____

_____

_____

_____

20...... _____

_____

_____

_____

_____

20...... _____

_____

_____

_____

_____

APRIL 23

20...... _____

_____

_____

_____

20...... _____

_____

_____

_____

20...... _____

_____

_____

_____

20...... _____

_____

_____

_____

20...... _____

_____

_____

_____

APRIL 24

20...... _____

_____

_____

_____

_____

20...... _____

_____

_____

_____

_____

20...... _____

_____

_____

_____

_____

20...... _____

_____

_____

_____

_____

20...... _____

_____

_____

_____

_____

APRIL 25

20...... _____

_____

_____

_____

_____

20...... _____

_____

_____

_____

_____

20...... _____

_____

_____

_____

_____

20...... _____

_____

_____

_____

_____

20...... _____

_____

_____

_____

_____

APRIL 26

20...... _____

_____

_____

_____

_____

20...... _____

_____

_____

_____

_____

20...... _____

_____

_____

_____

_____

20...... _____

_____

_____

_____

_____

20...... _____

_____

_____

_____

_____

APRIL 27

20...... _____

_____

_____

_____

20...... _____

_____

_____

_____

20...... _____

_____

_____

_____

20...... _____

_____

_____

_____

20...... _____

_____

_____

_____

APRIL 28

20...... _____

_____

_____

_____

_____

20...... _____

_____

_____

_____

_____

20...... _____

_____

_____

_____

_____

20...... _____

_____

_____

_____

_____

20...... _____

_____

_____

_____

_____

APRIL 29

20...... _____

_____

_____

_____

_____

20...... _____

_____

_____

_____

_____

20...... _____

_____

_____

_____

_____

20...... _____

_____

_____

_____

_____

20...... _____

_____

_____

_____

_____

APRIL 30

20......

_____

20......

_____

20......

_____

20......

_____

20......

_____

MAY 1

20...... _____

_____

_____

_____

20...... _____

_____

_____

_____

20...... _____

_____

_____

_____

20...... _____

_____

_____

_____

20...... _____

_____

_____

_____

20...... _____

_____

_____

_____

_____

20...... _____

_____

_____

_____

_____

20...... _____

_____

_____

_____

_____

20...... _____

_____

_____

_____

_____

20...... _____

_____

_____

_____

_____

MAY 3

20...... _____

_____

_____

_____

20...... _____

_____

_____

_____

20...... _____

_____

_____

_____

20...... _____

_____

_____

_____

20...... _____

_____

_____

_____

MAY 4

20......

_____

20......

_____

20......

_____

20......

_____

20......

_____

MAY 5

20...... _____
_____
_____
_____
_____

20...... _____
_____
_____
_____
_____

20...... _____
_____
_____
_____
_____

20...... _____
_____
_____
_____
_____

20...... _____
_____
_____
_____
_____

20......

_____

20......

_____

20......

_____

20......

_____

20......

_____

MAY 7

20...... _____

_____

_____

_____

_____

20...... _____

_____

_____

_____

_____

20...... _____

_____

_____

_____

_____

20...... _____

_____

_____

_____

_____

20...... _____

_____

_____

_____

_____

MAY 8

20...... _____

_____

_____

_____

_____

20...... _____

_____

_____

_____

_____

20...... _____

_____

_____

_____

_____

20...... _____

_____

_____

_____

_____

20...... _____

_____

_____

_____

_____

MAY 9

20...... _____

_____

_____

_____

_____

20...... _____

_____

_____

_____

_____

20...... _____

_____

_____

_____

_____

20...... _____

_____

_____

_____

_____

20...... _____

_____

_____

_____

_____

MAY 10

20...... _____

_____

_____

_____

_____

20...... _____

_____

_____

_____

_____

20...... _____

_____

_____

_____

_____

20...... _____

_____

_____

_____

_____

20...... _____

_____

_____

_____

_____

MAY 11

20...... _____
_____
_____
_____
_____

20...... _____
_____
_____
_____
_____

20...... _____
_____
_____
_____
_____

20...... _____
_____
_____
_____
_____

20...... _____
_____
_____
_____
_____

MAY 12

20......

20......

20......

20......

20......

MAY 13

20......

_____

20......

_____

20......

_____

20......

_____

20......

_____

MAY 14

20......

_____

20......

_____

20......

_____

20......

_____

20......

_____

MAY 15

20...... _____

20...... _____

20...... _____

20...... _____

20...... _____

MAY 16

20...... _____

_____

_____

_____

_____

20...... _____

_____

_____

_____

_____

20...... _____

_____

_____

_____

_____

20...... _____

_____

_____

_____

_____

20...... _____

_____

_____

_____

_____

20...... _____

_____

_____

_____

_____

20...... _____

_____

_____

_____

_____

20...... _____

_____

_____

_____

_____

20...... _____

_____

_____

_____

_____

20...... _____

_____

_____

_____

_____

MAY 18

20......

_____

_____

_____

_____

_____

20......

_____

_____

_____

_____

_____

20......

_____

_____

_____

_____

_____

20......

_____

_____

_____

_____

_____

20......

_____

_____

_____

_____

_____

MAY 19

20......

_____

_____

_____

_____

_____

20......

_____

_____

_____

_____

_____

20......

_____

_____

_____

_____

_____

20......

_____

_____

_____

_____

_____

20......

_____

_____

_____

_____

_____

MAY 20

20......

20......

20......

20......

20......

MAY 21

20...... _____

_____

_____

_____

20...... _____

_____

_____

_____

20...... _____

_____

_____

_____

20...... _____

_____

_____

_____

20...... _____

_____

_____

_____

MAY 22

20...... _____

_____

_____

_____

_____

20...... _____

_____

_____

_____

_____

20...... _____

_____

_____

_____

_____

20...... _____

_____

_____

_____

_____

20...... _____

_____

_____

_____

_____

MAY 23

20...... _____

_____

_____

_____

20...... _____

_____

_____

_____

20...... _____

_____

_____

_____

20...... _____

_____

_____

_____

20...... _____

_____

_____

_____

MAY 24

20...... _____

_____

_____

_____

_____

20...... _____

_____

_____

_____

_____

20...... _____

_____

_____

_____

_____

20...... _____

_____

_____

_____

_____

20...... _____

_____

_____

_____

_____

MAY 25

20...... _____
_____
_____
_____
_____

20...... _____
_____
_____
_____
_____

20...... _____
_____
_____
_____
_____

20...... _____
_____
_____
_____
_____

20...... _____
_____
_____
_____
_____

MAY 26

20......

_____

20......

_____

20......

_____

20......

_____

20......

MAY 27

20......

20......

20......

20......

20......

MAY 28

20......

20......

20......

20......

20......

MAY 29

20......

_____

20......

_____

20......

_____

20......

_____

20......

_____

MAY 30

20......

_____

20......

_____

20......

_____

20......

_____

20......

MAY 31

20...... _____

_____

_____

_____

_____

20...... _____

_____

_____

_____

_____

20...... _____

_____

_____

_____

_____

20...... _____

_____

_____

_____

_____

20...... _____

_____

_____

_____

_____

JUNE 1

20......

_____

20......

_____

20......

_____

20......

_____

20......

_____

JUNE 2

20...... _____

_____

_____

_____

_____

20...... _____

_____

_____

_____

_____

20...... _____

_____

_____

_____

_____

20...... _____

_____

_____

_____

_____

20...... _____

_____

_____

_____

_____

JUNE 3

20......

_____

20......

_____

20......

_____

20......

_____

20......

_____

JUNE 4

20...... _____

_____

_____

_____

_____

20...... _____

_____

_____

_____

_____

20...... _____

_____

_____

_____

_____

20...... _____

_____

_____

_____

_____

20...... _____

_____

_____

_____

_____

JUNE 5

20......

_____

20......

_____

20......

_____

20......

_____

20......

_____

JUNE 6

20...... _____

_____

_____

_____

_____

20...... _____

_____

_____

_____

_____

20...... _____

_____

_____

_____

_____

20...... _____

_____

_____

_____

_____

20...... _____

_____

_____

_____

_____

JUNE 7

20...... _____

_____

_____

_____

20...... _____

_____

_____

_____

20...... _____

_____

_____

_____

20...... _____

_____

_____

_____

20...... _____

_____

_____

_____

JUNE 8

20...... _____

_____

_____

_____

_____

20...... _____

_____

_____

_____

_____

20...... _____

_____

_____

_____

_____

20...... _____

_____

_____

_____

_____

20...... _____

_____

_____

_____

_____

JUNE 9

20......

20......

20......

20......

20......

JUNE 10

20...... _____

_____

_____

_____

_____

20...... _____

_____

_____

_____

_____

20...... _____

_____

_____

_____

_____

20...... _____

_____

_____

_____

_____

20...... _____

_____

_____

_____

_____

JUNE 11

20......

20......

20......

20......

20......

JUNE 12

20......

_____

20......

_____

20......

_____

20......

_____

20......

_____

JUNE 13

20...... _____

_____

_____

_____

20...... _____

_____

_____

_____

20...... _____

_____

_____

_____

20...... _____

_____

_____

_____

20...... _____

_____

_____

_____

JUNE 14

20...... _____
_____
_____
_____

20...... _____
_____
_____
_____

20...... _____
_____
_____
_____

20...... _____
_____
_____
_____

20...... _____
_____
_____
_____

JUNE 15

20...... _____

_____

_____

_____

_____

20...... _____

_____

_____

_____

_____

20...... _____

_____

_____

_____

_____

20...... _____

_____

_____

_____

_____

20...... _____

_____

_____

_____

_____

JUNE 16

20...... _____

_____

_____

_____

_____

20...... _____

_____

_____

_____

_____

20...... _____

_____

_____

_____

_____

20...... _____

_____

_____

_____

_____

20...... _____

_____

_____

_____

_____

JUNE 17

20......

_____

_____

_____

_____

20......

_____

_____

_____

_____

20......

_____

_____

_____

_____

20......

_____

_____

_____

_____

20......

_____

_____

_____

_____

JUNE 18

20...... _____

_____

_____

_____

_____

20...... _____

_____

_____

_____

_____

20...... _____

_____

_____

_____

_____

20...... _____

_____

_____

_____

_____

20...... _____

_____

_____

_____

_____

JUNE 19

20...... _____

_____

_____

_____

_____

20...... _____

_____

_____

_____

_____

20...... _____

_____

_____

_____

_____

20...... _____

_____

_____

_____

_____

20...... _____

_____

_____

_____

_____

JUNE 20

20...... _____

_____

_____

_____

_____

20...... _____

_____

_____

_____

_____

20...... _____

_____

_____

_____

_____

20...... _____

_____

_____

_____

_____

20...... _____

_____

_____

_____

_____

JUNE 21

20......
_____

20......
_____

20......
_____

20......
_____

20......
_____

JUNE 22

20......

_____

20......

_____

20......

_____

20......

_____

20......

_____

JUNE 23

20...... _____

_____

_____

_____

20...... _____

_____

_____

_____

20...... _____

_____

_____

_____

20...... _____

_____

_____

_____

20...... _____

_____

_____

_____

JUNE 24

20...... _____

_____

_____

_____

_____

20...... _____

_____

_____

_____

_____

20...... _____

_____

_____

_____

_____

20...... _____

_____

_____

_____

_____

20...... _____

_____

_____

_____

_____

JUNE 25

20...... _____

_____

_____

_____

_____

20...... _____

_____

_____

_____

_____

20...... _____

_____

_____

_____

_____

20...... _____

_____

_____

_____

_____

20...... _____

_____

_____

_____

_____

JUNE 26

20......

_____

20......

_____

20......

_____

20......

_____

20......

_____

JUNE 27

20...... _____

_____

_____

_____

20...... _____

_____

_____

_____

20...... _____

_____

_____

_____

20...... _____

_____

_____

_____

20...... _____

_____

_____

_____

JUNE 28

20...... _____

_____

_____

_____

20...... _____

_____

_____

_____

20...... _____

_____

_____

_____

20...... _____

_____

_____

_____

20...... _____

_____

_____

_____

JUNE 29

20...... _____

_____

_____

_____

_____

20...... _____

_____

_____

_____

_____

20...... _____

_____

_____

_____

_____

20...... _____

_____

_____

_____

_____

20...... _____

_____

_____

_____

_____

JUNE 30

20...... _____
_____
_____
_____
_____

20...... _____
_____
_____
_____
_____

20...... _____
_____
_____
_____
_____

20...... _____
_____
_____
_____
_____

20...... _____
_____
_____
_____
_____

JULY 1

20...... _____

_____

_____

_____

20...... _____

_____

_____

_____

20...... _____

_____

_____

_____

20...... _____

_____

_____

_____

20...... _____

_____

_____

_____

JULY 2

20...... _____

_____

_____

_____

_____

20...... _____

_____

_____

_____

_____

20...... _____

_____

_____

_____

_____

20...... _____

_____

_____

_____

_____

20...... _____

_____

_____

_____

_____

JULY 3

20...... _____

_____

_____

_____

_____

20...... _____

_____

_____

_____

_____

20...... _____

_____

_____

_____

_____

20...... _____

_____

_____

_____

_____

20...... _____

_____

_____

_____

_____

JULY 4

20...... _____

20...... _____

20...... _____

20...... _____

20...... _____

JULY 5

20......

20......

20......

20......

20......

JULY 6

20......

_____

_____

_____

_____

_____

20......

_____

_____

_____

_____

_____

20......

_____

_____

_____

_____

_____

20......

_____

_____

_____

_____

_____

20......

_____

_____

_____

_____

_____

JULY 7

20...... _____

_____

_____

_____

_____

20...... _____

_____

_____

_____

_____

20...... _____

_____

_____

_____

_____

20...... _____

_____

_____

_____

_____

20...... _____

_____

_____

_____

_____

JULY 8

20......

20......

20......

20......

20......

JULY 9

20......

20......

20......

20......

20......

JULY 10

20...... _____

_____

_____

_____

_____

20...... _____

_____

_____

_____

_____

20...... _____

_____

_____

_____

_____

20...... _____

_____

_____

_____

_____

20...... _____

_____

_____

_____

_____

JULY 11

20...... _____

_____

_____

_____

20...... _____

_____

_____

_____

20...... _____

_____

_____

_____

20...... _____

_____

_____

_____

20...... _____

_____

_____

_____

JULY 12

20......

20......

20......

20......

20......

JULY 13

20......

_____

_____

_____

_____

_____

20......

_____

_____

_____

_____

_____

20......

_____

_____

_____

_____

_____

20......

_____

_____

_____

_____

_____

20......

_____

_____

_____

_____

_____

JULY 14

20......

_____

20......

_____

20......

_____

20......

_____

20......

_____

JULY 15

20......

20......

20......

20......

20......

JULY 16

20......

_____

20......

_____

20......

_____

20......

_____

20......

_____

JULY 17

20...... _____

_____

_____

_____

_____

20...... _____

_____

_____

_____

_____

20...... _____

_____

_____

_____

_____

20...... _____

_____

_____

_____

_____

20...... _____

_____

_____

_____

_____

JULY 18

20......

_____

20......

_____

20......

_____

20......

_____

20......

_____

JULY 19

20......

_____

20......

_____

20......

_____

20......

_____

20......

_____

JULY 20

20...... _____
_____
_____
_____
_____

20...... _____
_____
_____
_____
_____

20...... _____
_____
_____
_____
_____

20...... _____
_____
_____
_____
_____

20...... _____
_____
_____
_____
_____

JULY 21

20...... _____

_____

_____

_____

_____

20...... _____

_____

_____

_____

_____

20...... _____

_____

_____

_____

_____

20...... _____

_____

_____

_____

_____

20...... _____

_____

_____

_____

_____

JULY 22

20......

_____

20......

_____

20......

_____

20......

_____

20......

_____

JULY 23

20...... _____

_____

_____

_____

_____

20...... _____

_____

_____

_____

_____

20...... _____

_____

_____

_____

_____

20...... _____

_____

_____

_____

_____

20...... _____

_____

_____

_____

_____

JULY 24

20...... _____

_____

_____

_____

_____

20...... _____

_____

_____

_____

_____

20...... _____

_____

_____

_____

_____

20...... _____

_____

_____

_____

_____

20...... _____

_____

_____

_____

_____

JULY 25

20......

_____

20......

_____

20......

_____

20......

_____

20......

_____

JULY 26

20...... _____

_____

_____

_____

20...... _____

_____

_____

_____

20...... _____

_____

_____

_____

20...... _____

_____

_____

_____

20...... _____

_____

_____

_____

JULY 27

20...... _____

_____

_____

_____

_____

20...... _____

_____

_____

_____

_____

20...... _____

_____

_____

_____

_____

20...... _____

_____

_____

_____

_____

20...... _____

_____

_____

_____

_____

JULY 28

20...... _____

_____

_____

_____

_____

20...... _____

_____

_____

_____

_____

20...... _____

_____

_____

_____

_____

20...... _____

_____

_____

_____

_____

20...... _____

_____

_____

_____

_____

JULY 29

20...... _____

_____

_____

_____

_____

20...... _____

_____

_____

_____

_____

20...... _____

_____

_____

_____

_____

20...... _____

_____

_____

_____

_____

20...... _____

_____

_____

_____

_____

JULY 30

20...... _____

_____

_____

_____

20...... _____

_____

_____

_____

20...... _____

_____

_____

_____

20...... _____

_____

_____

_____

20...... _____

_____

_____

_____

JULY 31

20...... _____

_____

_____

_____

_____

_____

20...... _____

_____

_____

_____

_____

_____

20...... _____

_____

_____

_____

_____

_____

20...... _____

_____

_____

_____

_____

_____

20...... _____

_____

_____

_____

_____

_____

AUGUST 1

20...... _____

_____

_____

_____

_____

20...... _____

_____

_____

_____

_____

20...... _____

_____

_____

_____

_____

20...... _____

_____

_____

_____

_____

20...... _____

_____

_____

_____

_____

AUGUST 2

20...... _____

_____

_____

_____

_____

20...... _____

_____

_____

_____

_____

20...... _____

_____

_____

_____

_____

20...... _____

_____

_____

_____

_____

20...... _____

_____

_____

_____

_____

AUGUST 3

20...... _____

_____

_____

_____

_____

20...... _____

_____

_____

_____

_____

20...... _____

_____

_____

_____

_____

20...... _____

_____

_____

_____

_____

20...... _____

_____

_____

_____

_____

AUGUST 4

20...... _____

_____

_____

_____

_____

20...... _____

_____

_____

_____

_____

20...... _____

_____

_____

_____

_____

20...... _____

_____

_____

_____

_____

20...... _____

_____

_____

_____

_____

AUGUST 5

20......

_____

20......

_____

20......

_____

20......

_____

20......

_____

AUGUST 6

20......

_____

20......

_____

20......

_____

20......

_____

20......

_____

AUGUST 7

20......

20......

20......

20......

20......

AUGUST 8

20...... _____

_____

_____

_____

_____

20...... _____

_____

_____

_____

_____

20...... _____

_____

_____

_____

_____

20...... _____

_____

_____

_____

_____

20...... _____

_____

_____

_____

_____

AUGUST 9

20...... _____

_____

_____

_____

_____

20...... _____

_____

_____

_____

_____

20...... _____

_____

_____

_____

_____

20...... _____

_____

_____

_____

_____

20...... _____

_____

_____

_____

_____

AUGUST 10

20...... _____

_____

_____

_____

_____

20...... _____

_____

_____

_____

_____

20...... _____

_____

_____

_____

_____

20...... _____

_____

_____

_____

_____

20...... _____

_____

_____

_____

_____

AUGUST 11

20...... _____

_____

_____

_____

_____

20...... _____

_____

_____

_____

_____

20...... _____

_____

_____

_____

_____

20...... _____

_____

_____

_____

_____

20...... _____

_____

_____

_____

_____

AUGUST 12

20...... _____

_____

_____

_____

_____

20...... _____

_____

_____

_____

_____

20...... _____

_____

_____

_____

_____

20...... _____

_____

_____

_____

_____

20...... _____

_____

_____

_____

_____

AUGUST 13

20...... _____

_____

_____

_____

_____

20...... _____

_____

_____

_____

_____

20...... _____

_____

_____

_____

_____

20...... _____

_____

_____

_____

_____

20...... _____

_____

_____

_____

_____

AUGUST 14

20......

_____

20......

_____

20......

_____

20......

_____

20......

_____

AUGUST 15

20...... _____
_____
_____
_____
_____

20...... _____
_____
_____
_____
_____

20...... _____
_____
_____
_____
_____

20...... _____
_____
_____
_____
_____

20...... _____
_____
_____
_____
_____

AUGUST 16

20...... _____

_____

_____

_____

20...... _____

_____

_____

_____

20...... _____

_____

_____

_____

20...... _____

_____

_____

_____

20...... _____

_____

_____

_____

AUGUST 17

20...... _____
_____
_____
_____
_____

20...... _____
_____
_____
_____
_____

20...... _____
_____
_____
_____
_____

20...... _____
_____
_____
_____
_____

20...... _____
_____
_____
_____
_____

AUGUST 18

20...... _____

_____

_____

_____

_____

20...... _____

_____

_____

_____

_____

20...... _____

_____

_____

_____

_____

20...... _____

_____

_____

_____

_____

20...... _____

_____

_____

_____

_____

AUGUST 19

20...... _____

_____

_____

_____

_____

20...... _____

_____

_____

_____

_____

20...... _____

_____

_____

_____

_____

20...... _____

_____

_____

_____

_____

20...... _____

_____

_____

_____

_____

AUGUST 20

20......

_____

20......

_____

20......

_____

20......

_____

20......

AUGUST 21

20......

_____

20......

_____

20......

_____

20......

_____

20......

_____

AUGUST 22

20...... _____

_____

_____

_____

_____

20...... _____

_____

_____

_____

_____

20...... _____

_____

_____

_____

_____

20...... _____

_____

_____

_____

_____

20...... _____

_____

_____

_____

_____

AUGUST 23

20...... _____

_____

_____

_____

_____

20...... _____

_____

_____

_____

_____

20...... _____

_____

_____

_____

_____

20...... _____

_____

_____

_____

_____

20...... _____

_____

_____

_____

_____

AUGUST 24

20...... _____

_____

_____

_____

_____

20...... _____

_____

_____

_____

_____

20...... _____

_____

_____

_____

_____

20...... _____

_____

_____

_____

_____

20...... _____

_____

_____

_____

_____

AUGUST 25

20...... _____

_____

_____

_____

_____

20...... _____

_____

_____

_____

_____

20...... _____

_____

_____

_____

_____

20...... _____

_____

_____

_____

_____

20...... _____

_____

_____

_____

_____

AUGUST 26

20...... _____

_____

_____

_____

_____

20...... _____

_____

_____

_____

_____

20...... _____

_____

_____

_____

_____

20...... _____

_____

_____

_____

_____

20...... _____

_____

_____

_____

_____

AUGUST 27

20...... _____

_____

_____

_____

_____

20...... _____

_____

_____

_____

_____

20...... _____

_____

_____

_____

_____

20...... _____

_____

_____

_____

_____

20...... _____

_____

_____

_____

_____

AUGUST 28

20......

20......

20......

20......

20......

AUGUST 29

20...... _____

_____

_____

_____

20...... _____

_____

_____

_____

20...... _____

_____

_____

_____

20...... _____

_____

_____

_____

20...... _____

_____

_____

_____

AUGUST 30

20...... _____

_____

_____

_____

_____

20...... _____

_____

_____

_____

_____

20...... _____

_____

_____

_____

_____

20...... _____

_____

_____

_____

_____

20...... _____

_____

_____

_____

_____

AUGUST 31

20...... _____

_____

_____

_____

_____

20...... _____

_____

_____

_____

_____

20...... _____

_____

_____

_____

_____

20...... _____

_____

_____

_____

_____

20...... _____

_____

_____

_____

_____

SEPTEMBER 1

20......

_____

20......

_____

20......

_____

20......

_____

20......

_____

20...... _____
_____
_____
_____
_____

20...... _____
_____
_____
_____
_____

20...... _____
_____
_____
_____
_____

20...... _____
_____
_____
_____
_____

20...... _____
_____
_____
_____
_____

SEPTEMBER 3

20......

_____

20......

_____

20......

_____

20......

_____

20......

_____

SEPTEMBER 4

20......

_____

20......

_____

20......

_____

20......

_____

20......

_____

SEPTEMBER 5

20......

_____

_____

_____

_____

_____

20......

_____

_____

_____

_____

_____

20......

_____

_____

_____

_____

_____

20......

_____

_____

_____

_____

_____

20......

_____

_____

_____

_____

_____

SEPTEMBER 6

20...... _____

_____

_____

_____

_____

20...... _____

_____

_____

_____

_____

20...... _____

_____

_____

_____

_____

20...... _____

_____

_____

_____

_____

20...... _____

_____

_____

_____

_____

SEPTEMBER 7

20......

_____

20......

_____

20......

_____

20......

_____

20......

SEPTEMBER 8

20......

_____

20......

_____

20......

_____

20......

_____

20......

_____

SEPTEMBER 9

20......

_____

_____

_____

_____

_____

20......

_____

_____

_____

_____

_____

20......

_____

_____

_____

_____

_____

20......

_____

_____

_____

_____

_____

20......

_____

_____

_____

_____

_____

SEPTEMBER 10

20......

_____

20......

_____

20......

_____

20......

_____

20......

_____

SEPTEMBER 11

20......

20......

20......

20......

20......

SEPTEMBER 12

20...... _____

_____

_____

_____

_____

20...... _____

_____

_____

_____

_____

20...... _____

_____

_____

_____

_____

20...... _____

_____

_____

_____

_____

20...... _____

_____

_____

_____

_____

20......

_____

_____

_____

_____

_____

20......

_____

_____

_____

_____

_____

20......

_____

_____

_____

_____

_____

20......

_____

_____

_____

_____

_____

20......

_____

_____

_____

_____

_____

SEPTEMBER 14

20...... _____

_____

_____

_____

_____

20...... _____

_____

_____

_____

_____

20...... _____

_____

_____

_____

_____

20...... _____

_____

_____

_____

_____

20...... _____

_____

_____

_____

_____

20...... _____

_____

_____

_____

_____

20...... _____

_____

_____

_____

_____

20...... _____

_____

_____

_____

_____

20...... _____

_____

_____

_____

_____

20...... _____

_____

_____

_____

_____

SEPTEMBER 16

20...... _____

_____

_____

_____

_____

20...... _____

_____

_____

_____

_____

20...... _____

_____

_____

_____

_____

20...... _____

_____

_____

_____

_____

20...... _____

_____

_____

_____

_____

20......

_____

20......

_____

20......

_____

20......

_____

20......

20...... _____

_____

_____

_____

_____

20...... _____

_____

_____

_____

_____

20...... _____

_____

_____

_____

_____

20...... _____

_____

_____

_____

_____

20...... _____

_____

_____

_____

_____

SEPTEMBER 19

20...... _____

_____

_____

_____

_____

20...... _____

_____

_____

_____

_____

20...... _____

_____

_____

_____

_____

20...... _____

_____

_____

_____

_____

20...... _____

_____

_____

_____

_____

20...... _____

_____

_____

_____

_____

20...... _____

_____

_____

_____

_____

20...... _____

_____

_____

_____

_____

20...... _____

_____

_____

_____

_____

20...... _____

_____

_____

_____

_____

20......

20......

20......

20......

20......

SEPTEMBER 22

20...... _____

_____

_____

_____

_____

20...... _____

_____

_____

_____

_____

20...... _____

_____

_____

_____

_____

20...... _____

_____

_____

_____

_____

20...... _____

_____

_____

_____

_____

SEPTEMBER 23

20......

20......

20......

20......

20......

SEPTEMBER 24

20...... _____

_____

_____

_____

_____

20...... _____

_____

_____

_____

_____

20...... _____

_____

_____

_____

_____

20...... _____

_____

_____

_____

_____

20...... _____

_____

_____

_____

_____

20...... _____

_____

_____

_____

_____

20...... _____

_____

_____

_____

_____

20...... _____

_____

_____

_____

_____

20...... _____

_____

_____

_____

_____

20...... _____

_____

_____

_____

_____

SEPTEMBER 26

20......

_____

_____

_____

_____

_____

20......

_____

_____

_____

_____

_____

20......

_____

_____

_____

_____

_____

20......

_____

_____

_____

_____

_____

20......

_____

_____

_____

_____

_____

SEPTEMBER 27

20......

20......

20......

20......

20......

SEPTEMBER 28

20......

_____

20......

_____

20......

_____

20......

_____

20......

20......

_____

20......

_____

20......

_____

20......

_____

20......

_____

SEPTEMBER 30

20...... _____

_____

_____

_____

_____

20...... _____

_____

_____

_____

_____

20...... _____

_____

_____

_____

_____

20...... _____

_____

_____

_____

_____

20...... _____

_____

_____

_____

_____

OCTOBER 1

20...... _____

_____

_____

_____

_____

20...... _____

_____

_____

_____

_____

20...... _____

_____

_____

_____

_____

20...... _____

_____

_____

_____

_____

20...... _____

_____

_____

_____

_____

OCTOBER 2

20......

_____

20......

_____

20......

_____

20......

_____

20......

OCTOBER 3

20...... _____

_____

_____

_____

_____

20...... _____

_____

_____

_____

_____

20...... _____

_____

_____

_____

_____

20...... _____

_____

_____

_____

_____

20...... _____

_____

_____

_____

_____

OCTOBER 4

20......

_____

20......

_____

20......

_____

20......

_____

20......

OCTOBER 5

20......

_____

20......

_____

20......

_____

20......

_____

20......

_____

OCTOBER 6

20......

_____

20......

_____

20......

_____

20......

_____

20......

_____

OCTOBER 7

20......

_____

20......

_____

20......

_____

20......

_____

20......

_____

OCTOBER 8

20...... _____

_____

_____

_____

_____

20...... _____

_____

_____

_____

_____

20...... _____

_____

_____

_____

_____

20...... _____

_____

_____

_____

_____

20...... _____

_____

_____

_____

_____

OCTOBER 9

20...... _____

_____

_____

_____

_____

20...... _____

_____

_____

_____

_____

20...... _____

_____

_____

_____

_____

20...... _____

_____

_____

_____

_____

20...... _____

_____

_____

_____

_____

OCTOBER 10

20...... _____

_____

_____

_____

_____

20...... _____

_____

_____

_____

_____

20...... _____

_____

_____

_____

_____

20...... _____

_____

_____

_____

_____

20...... _____

_____

_____

_____

_____

OCTOBER 11

20......

_____

20......

_____

20......

_____

20......

_____

20......

_____

OCTOBER 12

20...... _____

_____

_____

_____

20...... _____

_____

_____

_____

20...... _____

_____

_____

_____

20...... _____

_____

_____

_____

20...... _____

_____

_____

_____

20......

_____

20......

_____

20......

_____

20......

_____

20......

OCTOBER 14

20......

_____

20......

_____

20......

_____

20......

_____

20......

_____

OCTOBER 15

20...... _____

_____

_____

_____

_____

20...... _____

_____

_____

_____

_____

20...... _____

_____

_____

_____

_____

20...... _____

_____

_____

_____

_____

20...... _____

_____

_____

_____

_____

OCTOBER 16

20...... _____
_____
_____
_____
_____

20...... _____
_____
_____
_____
_____

20...... _____
_____
_____
_____
_____

20...... _____
_____
_____
_____
_____

20...... _____
_____
_____
_____
_____

20......

_____

_____

_____

_____

_____

20......

_____

_____

_____

_____

_____

20......

_____

_____

_____

_____

_____

20......

_____

_____

_____

_____

_____

20......

_____

_____

_____

_____

_____

OCTOBER 18

20...... _____
_____
_____
_____
_____

20...... _____
_____
_____
_____
_____

20...... _____
_____
_____
_____
_____

20...... _____
_____
_____
_____
_____

20...... _____
_____
_____
_____
_____

OCTOBER 19

20...... _____

_____

_____

_____

_____

20...... _____

_____

_____

_____

_____

20...... _____

_____

_____

_____

_____

20...... _____

_____

_____

_____

_____

20...... _____

_____

_____

_____

_____

OCTOBER 20

20......

_____

20......

_____

20......

_____

20......

_____

20......

OCTOBER 21

20......

_____

20......

_____

20......

_____

20......

_____

20......

_____

OCTOBER 22

20...... _____

_____

_____

_____

_____

20...... _____

_____

_____

_____

_____

20...... _____

_____

_____

_____

_____

20...... _____

_____

_____

_____

_____

20...... _____

_____

_____

_____

_____

OCTOBER 23

20...... _____

_____

_____

_____

_____

20...... _____

_____

_____

_____

_____

20...... _____

_____

_____

_____

_____

20...... _____

_____

_____

_____

_____

20...... _____

_____

_____

_____

_____

OCTOBER 24

20...... _____

_____

_____

_____

20...... _____

_____

_____

_____

20...... _____

_____

_____

_____

20...... _____

_____

_____

_____

20...... _____

_____

_____

_____

OCTOBER 25

20......

_____

20......

_____

20......

_____

20......

_____

20......

OCTOBER 26

20......

20......

20......

20......

20......

OCTOBER 27

20......

_____

20......

_____

20......

_____

20......

_____

20......

_____

OCTOBER 28

20...... _____

20...... _____

20...... _____

20...... _____

20...... _____

OCTOBER 29

20......

_____

20......

_____

20......

_____

20......

_____

20......

OCTOBER 30

20...... _____

_____

_____

_____

_____

20...... _____

_____

_____

_____

_____

20...... _____

_____

_____

_____

_____

20...... _____

_____

_____

_____

_____

20...... _____

_____

_____

_____

_____

OCTOBER 31

20......

_____

_____

_____

_____

_____

20......

_____

_____

_____

_____

_____

20......

_____

_____

_____

_____

_____

20......

_____

_____

_____

_____

_____

20......

_____

_____

_____

_____

_____

NOVEMBER 1

20...... _____
_____
_____
_____
_____

20...... _____
_____
_____
_____
_____

20...... _____
_____
_____
_____
_____

20...... _____
_____
_____
_____
_____

20...... _____
_____
_____
_____
_____

NOVEMBER 2

20...... _____

_____

_____

_____

_____

20...... _____

_____

_____

_____

_____

20...... _____

_____

_____

_____

_____

20...... _____

_____

_____

_____

_____

20...... _____

_____

_____

_____

_____

NOVEMBER 3

20......

_____

20......

_____

20......

_____

20......

_____

20......

_____

NOVEMBER 4

20...... _____

_____

_____

_____

_____

20...... _____

_____

_____

_____

_____

20...... _____

_____

_____

_____

_____

20...... _____

_____

_____

_____

_____

20...... _____

_____

_____

_____

_____

NOVEMBER 5

20...... _____

_____

_____

_____

_____

20...... _____

_____

_____

_____

_____

20...... _____

_____

_____

_____

_____

20...... _____

_____

_____

_____

_____

20...... _____

_____

_____

_____

_____

NOVEMBER 6

20...... _____

_____

_____

_____

_____

20...... _____

_____

_____

_____

_____

20...... _____

_____

_____

_____

_____

20...... _____

_____

_____

_____

_____

20...... _____

_____

_____

_____

_____

NOVEMBER 7

20...... _____

_____

_____

_____

20...... _____

_____

_____

_____

20...... _____

_____

_____

_____

20...... _____

_____

_____

_____

20...... _____

_____

_____

_____

NOVEMBER 8

20......

20......

20......

20......

20......

NOVEMBER 9

20...... _____

_____

_____

_____

_____

20...... _____

_____

_____

_____

_____

20...... _____

_____

_____

_____

_____

20...... _____

_____

_____

_____

_____

20...... _____

_____

_____

_____

_____

NOVEMBER 10

20...... _____

_____

_____

_____

_____

20...... _____

_____

_____

_____

_____

20...... _____

_____

_____

_____

_____

20...... _____

_____

_____

_____

_____

20...... _____

_____

_____

_____

_____

NOVEMBER 11

20...... _____
_____
_____
_____
_____

20...... _____
_____
_____
_____
_____

20...... _____
_____
_____
_____
_____

20...... _____
_____
_____
_____
_____

20...... _____
_____
_____
_____
_____

NOVEMBER 12

20...... _____

_____

_____

_____

_____

20...... _____

_____

_____

_____

_____

20...... _____

_____

_____

_____

_____

20...... _____

_____

_____

_____

_____

20...... _____

_____

_____

_____

_____

NOVEMBER 13

20...... _____

_____

_____

_____

_____

20...... _____

_____

_____

_____

_____

20...... _____

_____

_____

_____

_____

20...... _____

_____

_____

_____

_____

20...... _____

_____

_____

_____

_____

20...... _____

_____

_____

_____

_____

20...... _____

_____

_____

_____

_____

20...... _____

_____

_____

_____

_____

20...... _____

_____

_____

_____

_____

20...... _____

_____

_____

_____

_____

NOVEMBER 15

20...... _____

_____

_____

_____

20...... _____

_____

_____

_____

20...... _____

_____

_____

_____

20...... _____

_____

_____

_____

20...... _____

_____

_____

_____

20...... _____
_____
_____
_____
_____

20...... _____
_____
_____
_____
_____

20...... _____
_____
_____
_____
_____

20...... _____
_____
_____
_____
_____

20...... _____
_____
_____
_____
_____

20...... _____
_____
_____
_____
_____

20...... _____
_____
_____
_____
_____

20...... _____
_____
_____
_____
_____

20...... _____
_____
_____
_____
_____

20...... _____
_____
_____
_____
_____

NOVEMBER 18

20......
_____

20......
_____

20......
_____

20......
_____

20......
_____

20...... _____

_____

_____

_____

_____

20...... _____

_____

_____

_____

_____

20...... _____

_____

_____

_____

_____

20...... _____

_____

_____

_____

_____

20...... _____

_____

_____

_____

_____

20...... _____

_____

_____

_____

_____

20...... _____

_____

_____

_____

_____

20...... _____

_____

_____

_____

_____

20...... _____

_____

_____

_____

_____

20...... _____

_____

_____

_____

_____

NOVEMBER 21

20...... _____

_____

_____

_____

20...... _____

_____

_____

_____

20...... _____

_____

_____

_____

20...... _____

_____

_____

_____

20...... _____

_____

_____

_____

NOVEMBER 22

20...... _____

_____

_____

_____

_____

20...... _____

_____

_____

_____

_____

20...... _____

_____

_____

_____

_____

20...... _____

_____

_____

_____

_____

20...... _____

_____

_____

_____

_____

20...... _____

_____

_____

_____

_____

20...... _____

_____

_____

_____

_____

20...... _____

_____

_____

_____

_____

20...... _____

_____

_____

_____

_____

20...... _____

_____

_____

_____

_____

NOVEMBER 24

20...... _____

_____

_____

_____

_____

20...... _____

_____

_____

_____

_____

20...... _____

_____

_____

_____

_____

20...... _____

_____

_____

_____

_____

20...... _____

_____

_____

_____

_____

NOVEMBER 25

20......

_____

20......

_____

20......

_____

20......

_____

20......

_____

NOVEMBER 26

20......

20......

20......

20......

20......

20......

_____

20......

_____

20......

_____

20......

_____

20......

_____

NOVEMBER 28

20...... _____

_____

_____

_____

_____

20...... _____

_____

_____

_____

_____

20...... _____

_____

_____

_____

_____

20...... _____

_____

_____

_____

_____

20...... _____

_____

_____

_____

_____

20...... _____
_____
_____
_____
_____

20...... _____
_____
_____
_____
_____

20...... _____
_____
_____
_____
_____

20...... _____
_____
_____
_____
_____

20...... _____
_____
_____
_____
_____

NOVEMBER 30

20......

_____

20......

_____

20......

_____

20......

_____

20......

_____

DECEMBER 1

20...... _____

_____

_____

_____

_____

20...... _____

_____

_____

_____

_____

20...... _____

_____

_____

_____

_____

20...... _____

_____

_____

_____

_____

20...... _____

_____

_____

_____

_____

DECEMBER 2

20......

_____

_____

_____

_____

_____

20......

_____

_____

_____

_____

_____

20......

_____

_____

_____

_____

_____

20......

_____

_____

_____

_____

_____

20......

_____

_____

_____

_____

_____

DECEMBER 3

20...... _____

_____

_____

_____

_____

20...... _____

_____

_____

_____

_____

20...... _____

_____

_____

_____

_____

20...... _____

_____

_____

_____

_____

20...... _____

_____

_____

_____

_____

DECEMBER 4

20......

_____

_____

_____

_____

20......

_____

_____

_____

_____

20......

_____

_____

_____

_____

20......

_____

_____

_____

_____

20......

_____

_____

_____

_____

DECEMBER 5

20......

_____

20......

_____

20......

_____

20......

_____

20......

_____

DECEMBER 6

20...... _____

_____

_____

_____

_____

20...... _____

_____

_____

_____

_____

20...... _____

_____

_____

_____

_____

20...... _____

_____

_____

_____

_____

20...... _____

_____

_____

_____

_____

DECEMBER 7

20...... _____

_____

_____

_____

_____

20...... _____

_____

_____

_____

_____

20...... _____

_____

_____

_____

_____

20...... _____

_____

_____

_____

_____

20...... _____

_____

_____

_____

_____

DECEMBER 8

20...... _____

_____

_____

_____

_____

20...... _____

_____

_____

_____

_____

20...... _____

_____

_____

_____

_____

20...... _____

_____

_____

_____

_____

20...... _____

_____

_____

_____

_____

DECEMBER 9

20......

_____

_____

_____

_____

_____

20......

_____

_____

_____

_____

_____

20......

_____

_____

_____

_____

_____

20......

_____

_____

_____

_____

_____

20......

_____

_____

_____

_____

_____

DECEMBER 10

20...... _____

_____

_____

_____

_____

20...... _____

_____

_____

_____

_____

20...... _____

_____

_____

_____

_____

20...... _____

_____

_____

_____

_____

20...... _____

_____

_____

_____

_____

DECEMBER 11

20......

_____

20......

_____

20......

_____

20......

_____

20......

DECEMBER 12

20...... _____

_____

_____

_____

_____

20...... _____

_____

_____

_____

_____

20...... _____

_____

_____

_____

_____

20...... _____

_____

_____

_____

_____

20...... _____

_____

_____

_____

_____

DECEMBER 13

20...... _____

_____

_____

_____

_____

20...... _____

_____

_____

_____

_____

20...... _____

_____

_____

_____

_____

20...... _____

_____

_____

_____

_____

20...... _____

_____

_____

_____

_____

DECEMBER 14

20......
_____
_____
_____
_____

20......
_____
_____
_____
_____

20......
_____
_____
_____
_____

20......
_____
_____
_____
_____

20......
_____
_____
_____
_____

DECEMBER 15

20...... _____

_____

_____

_____

_____

20...... _____

_____

_____

_____

_____

20...... _____

_____

_____

_____

_____

20...... _____

_____

_____

_____

_____

20...... _____

_____

_____

_____

_____

DECEMBER 16

20......

_____

20......

_____

20......

_____

20......

_____

20......

_____

DECEMBER 17

20...... _____

_____

_____

_____

_____

20...... _____

_____

_____

_____

_____

20...... _____

_____

_____

_____

_____

20...... _____

_____

_____

_____

_____

20...... _____

_____

_____

_____

_____

DECEMBER 18

20...... _____

_____

_____

_____

_____

20...... _____

_____

_____

_____

_____

20...... _____

_____

_____

_____

_____

20...... _____

_____

_____

_____

_____

20...... _____

_____

_____

_____

_____

DECEMBER 19

20......

_____

20......

_____

20......

_____

20......

_____

20......

_____

DECEMBER 20

20...... _____

_____

_____

_____

_____

20...... _____

_____

_____

_____

_____

20...... _____

_____

_____

_____

_____

20...... _____

_____

_____

_____

_____

20...... _____

_____

_____

_____

_____

DECEMBER 21

20...... _____

_____

_____

_____

_____

20...... _____

_____

_____

_____

_____

20...... _____

_____

_____

_____

_____

20...... _____

_____

_____

_____

_____

20...... _____

_____

_____

_____

_____

DECEMBER 22

20...... _____

_____

_____

_____

_____

20...... _____

_____

_____

_____

_____

20...... _____

_____

_____

_____

_____

20...... _____

_____

_____

_____

_____

20...... _____

_____

_____

_____

_____

DECEMBER 23

20...... _____

_____

_____

_____

_____

20...... _____

_____

_____

_____

_____

20...... _____

_____

_____

_____

_____

20...... _____

_____

_____

_____

_____

20...... _____

_____

_____

_____

_____

DECEMBER 24

20...... _____

_____

_____

_____

_____

20...... _____

_____

_____

_____

_____

20...... _____

_____

_____

_____

_____

20...... _____

_____

_____

_____

_____

20...... _____

_____

_____

_____

_____

DECEMBER 25

20...... _____

_____

_____

_____

_____

20...... _____

_____

_____

_____

_____

20...... _____

_____

_____

_____

_____

20...... _____

_____

_____

_____

_____

20...... _____

_____

_____

_____

_____

DECEMBER 26

20......

_____

20......

_____

20......

_____

20......

_____

20......

DECEMBER 27

20...... _____
_____
_____
_____
_____

20...... _____
_____
_____
_____
_____

20...... _____
_____
_____
_____
_____

20...... _____
_____
_____
_____
_____

20...... _____
_____
_____
_____
_____

DECEMBER 28

20......

_____

20......

_____

20......

_____

20......

_____

20......

_____

DECEMBER 29

20...... _____

_____

_____

_____

_____

20...... _____

_____

_____

_____

_____

20...... _____

_____

_____

_____

_____

20...... _____

_____

_____

_____

_____

20...... _____

_____

_____

_____

_____

DECEMBER 30

20......

_____

_____

_____

_____

20......

_____

_____

_____

_____

20......

_____

_____

_____

_____

20......

_____

_____

_____

_____

20......

_____

_____

_____

_____

DECEMBER 31

20...... _____

_____

_____

_____

_____

20...... _____

_____

_____

_____

_____

20...... _____

_____

_____

_____

_____

20...... _____

_____

_____

_____

_____

20...... _____

_____

_____

_____

_____

ONE LINE A DAY

A Five Year Memory Book

WILDERTHOUGHTS.COM

Made in the USA
Las Vegas, NV
24 November 2021

35249187R00203